Set Of Poems On Several Original, Important, Interesting, And Sweet Topics

By Fernando Penagos

Contents

Dedication

To my lovely Grandma Rosa, whose kindness, wisdom, and warmth fill my heart with joy. Your words, your laughter, and your love inspire me every day. This is for you—my greatest supporter, my sweetest friend.

About the Author

For 12 years, Fernando Penagos has found strength, support, and a true sense of belonging at the Somerville YMCA—a place he proudly calls his second home.

Born on December 25, 1982, Fernando once struggled with weight and high cholesterol. At the urging of a family member, he joined the Y and embraced a dedicated fitness routine, working out 3 to 4 hours per session, 4 to 5 days a week. He takes full advantage of the Y's wellness programs—running on the treadmill, hitting the boxing bag, biking, and, most of all, swimming. Beyond fitness, he cherishes the friendships and encouragement that make the Y feel like family.

Swimming has become his passion and a key part of his journey. He diligently tracks his progress, recently completing 800 laps in two weeks and surpassing 8,593 laps between last year and July 2021.

Academically, Fernando has also excelled. He graduated from County College of Morris in May 2018 with an 'A-' average, earning a spot on the Dean's Honors List four times. In May 2023, he completed his degree at Rutgers University with a 'B+' average, making the Dean's List four times. While his academic journey is complete, his commitment to fitness remains strong, and he continues to enjoy exercising at various YMCAs, especially swimming.

"The Y isn't just a gym—it's a place that has shaped my life. The staff genuinely care, always encouraging me to reach my goals. Thanks to the Y, I've improved my health, built discipline, and found a supportive community. It's a part of who I am."

Poem & Song Dedicated To
My Lovely Grandma Rosa

Rosa is my grandmother
Who says I am smart
We care for each other
And are enormous at heart

Her Spanish fills me with joy
She has a great voice
It is as fine as a toy
Which makes me rejoice

Her favorite color's white
Mine is the green
What a wonderful sight
And is totally keen

She is fond of the rose
As she can truly tell
It strikes a great pose
That sounds so swell

I love my grandmother
The beauty's so sweet
We adore one another
And will always meet

Spanish is her tone
It fills me with pride
As I use my own
That opens up wide

Rosa is very kind
Her looks are quite dandy
The ties will bind
As nice as candy

With me as her grandson
We will show much love
Which are loads of fun
Just as the cooing of a dove

Special Birthday Poem For My Mom

Happy birthday to my mother
Who is pretty and sweet
We happily love each other
And do our best to meet

She is as nice as candy
Beautiful as many flowers
Our Spanish talk is very handy
Which is all ours

Helping her is a big thing that I have done
She has deeply relied on me
With the support as her son
As we can clearly see

I will continue doing all on my part
For my one and only mother
So, she has a special place in my heart
And we will always adore one another

Special Poem For
My Parents' Anniversary

Happy anniversary to my mom and dad
They're the ones who I adore
I have made them very proud, happy, and glad
With all I have done, they will surely ask for more

My folks have been with me for years
We have helped each other for so long
Their voices in Spanish are music to my ears
This language that we have spoken is like one big song

They have raised me with much care
We bond together in glee
Our big support comes from here and there
The nicer we treat ourselves, the more it's as us feeling
free

With me as their loving and caring son
Admiration and love are what will be shown
Everything between us can continue as fun
And we will always be very well-known

Fun Poem All About Birthdays

Birthday parties and presents galore
Filled with much cheer and fun
Joy and laughter more and more
Meant to send thrills to everyone

Cake and ice cream for delights
Gifts for every honored girl and boy
Whether taking place on days or nights
Everything from cards, clothes, to a fun toy

Celebrations complete with every guest
Entertainment including games and the birthday song
Where the event is set to be the best
For all times either short or long

Occasions done on any 365th day of the year
With everybody doing all their parts
Special moments loaded with total cheer
And meant to warm plenty of people's hearts

Birthdays, birthdays, all around
Coming from here and there
Especially with a bunch of joyful sound
Bringing up lots and lots of care

Special Poem About Valentine's Day

Valentine's Day, we adore you in every way
With our many hugs and kisses
You send out love on this day
To every Mr. and Mrs.

Your sweetness fills us with pride
Keep showing us your red, pink, and white
That will stay at our side
It is a joyous sight

Give us all your tasty chocolate candy
Continue growing beautiful flowers
Those will be very dandy
And continue being all ours

Do what you can so we can rejoice
Love is a many splendored thing
This has an admirable voice
Which will make us sing

February 14th is our day for love
That will make us full of joy
Just as the sound of a dove
And as wonderful as a toy

Amazing Poem About Easter

Hip, hip, hooray for a terrific and special Sunday
It's a very wonderful and fine time of the year
That is called Easter in a truly remarkable way
And is filled with plenty and plenty of cheer

It also calls for the cute bunny that spreads joy
Who goes around giving out colored eggs and candy
This is really meant for every good little girl and boy
Even donated chocolate treats are considered very
dandy

All sweets are put in lovely baskets made of paper or
straw
Which can come in many colors like brown, yellow,
and white
Each of these tasty treats are for satisfying a
mouthwatering jaw
Everything about this big terrific holiday is a most
precious sight

Whether taking place in the third or fourth month of
the year
This time can truly trigger many kids and adults being
merry
Celebrations of the day will bring all those from far
and near
All foods for the feast here will be as flavorful as a
fruity red cherry

Wonderful Poem About Mother's Day

Mother's Day is lovely for all the Mrs.
Which is meant to give them a darling present
This includes a lot of hugs and kisses
And makes the occasion very pleasant

It goes for every aunt, grandma, sister, and mother
Followed by their children's and husbands' love
That is spread out to each other
Just as the call of the morning white dove

Gifts include adorable cards and flowers
Jewelry can come close by
All families can have fun for hours
Without a moment of ever being shy

With this event always occurring in May
Many females will be delighted with glee
Their respected ones truly picture this special day
As one with everybody feeling very lively and free

Wonderful Poem About Father's Day

Let's hear it for the month of June
To honor every uncle, grandpa, brother, and dad
For Father's Day even by the light of the moon
And to feel ever so merry and glad

Our males teach life very well
They're meant to support us every day
How they do it, only time will tell
Every adult him is here to stay

Fathers, fathers, everywhere
Give everyone the love they need
As well as lots and lots of care
Which never includes any greed

Male relatives from all around
Are ones that we should admire
They are always in any place to be found
Having them can help kids inspire

This holiday is one to warm anyone's heart
Every child can learn from their dad
They can eventually become very smart
And be sure to never turn sad

Composition For Independence Day

4th of July, a very important date
Three cheers for the red, white, and blue
Pride brought to every state
And U.S. people, too

Independence Day, fill your spaces
Spread freedom throughout our land
All Americans, show your faces
And join in a patriotic band

Our soldiers and presidents have been bold
Their work has been so true
Fort Knox is their reserve of gold
As we the people know, too

Monuments and buildings, expose your pride
Keep showing us all your need
Stay at our whole side
To give us your importance indeed

4th of July, bring your fame
Please provide us with glory
We admire you all the same
Do your best to remain our top story

Terrific Poem About Parents Day

Let's hear it for our 7th month of the year
To give thanks to every mom and dad
And supply them with a lot of cheer
For Parents Day to make them merry and glad

This day is also meant for each daughter and son
As their folks have raised them well
Every day includes loads of fun
Like each family can easily tell

Mothers and fathers delightfully join
Along with all girls and boys
The event is as shiny as a silver coin
Which brings plenty of joys

The holiday is for every husband and wife
Who love their many young ones
And is a wonderful part in life
For parents and kids of tons

Admirable Poem About Grandparents' Day

Three cheers for our month of September
By providing much love and care
For a day that we all remember
To grandfathers and grandmothers everywhere

Such a wonderful time for all elders young and old
Including each granddaughter and grandson
An event that is never meant to feel cold
And should be treated with lots of fun

Grandparents come from all around
To be with everyone they adore
Kids and grandkids can easily be found
Celebrating via one big musical score

Bless every grandma and grandpa far and near
On this very special family holiday
Which brings them endless cheer
With complete shouts of hip, hip, hooray

Great Poem About Halloween

Let's hear it for the tenth month of the year
For an enjoyable and scary time that falls on the last
day
Which certainly calls for some fright as well as cheer
Halloween is this time as all the people say

A pumpkin is the fruit that is for most need
The colors for this event are orange and black
Kids in costumes go for candy without any greed
The phrase "trick-or-treat" is necessary for each child's
sack

Jack-o-lanterns are set up as the most common light
Decorations include images of monsters and a witch
Mummies and skeletons indicate a joyful but chilling
night
Music from organs can be played and heard with a
strong pitch

The evening of October 31st is meant for horror and
fun
Every moment is either incredibly good or terrifyingly
bad
This will go for every adult with their daughter or son
Even with their many costumes and treats, nobody will
ever be sad

Wonderful Poem About Thanksgiving

Three cheers for month number eleven
For a very special day that comes by
It makes us all feel like we are in heaven
That is called Thanksgiving which will never die

Those who join together include families and friends
People from all around do their best to always meet
With this exciting holiday occurring, the fun never
ends
This event comes with lots and lots of food to eat

Everyone comes from the south, north, west, and east
It's a time that calls for one extremely big turkey
dinner
Much cuisine for this day is added to the enormous
feast
All Americans who attend the festivity are considered
a winner

Some dishes include mashed potatoes and candied
yams
Desserts for Thanksgiving are ones such as pumpkin
pie
Other choices are cranberries as well as steamed hams
There are several different things here for you to try

Here is a holiday that you will always treasure
You can make your one wish when you are done
It has been and still is an honor as well as pleasure
For a day that is definitely loads and loads of fun

Lovely Poem About Christmas

Christmas is as good as here
Filled with happiness and joy
With Santa bringing cheer
To every girl and boy

A day full of red and green
Ready everywhere to go
All sights great and keen
And Mr. Claus shouting ho, ho, ho

Each toy done by him and his elves
From his own workshop
Be ready to enjoy yourselves
As he makes each stop

Delight and love come this day
Complete with every present
Celebrated in every way
Which makes it very pleasant

December 25th is very, very, true
Full of much glee and cheer
So, we wish all of you
A Merry Christmas and Happy New Year

Fun Poem About Pinball

Pinball, an extremely fun and nice game
One that is found at every video arcade
Points are scored differently or the same
Its machines are the greatest ever made

There are bumpers that are all around
One flipper is on both the left and right
Each ball that is played makes great sound
Earning bonus points in this is a great sight

The main buttons for control are on each side
There is also one for launching three balls per play
With the popular game, they take a very fun ride
Whether people enjoy it at night or during the day

Adults and kids really love the activity of pinball
That is yet another thing that is loads and loads of fun
No matter where it is located, this will be played by all
With careful planning, even winning a free game can
be done

Poem Created For Admirers Of Playing Cards

Cards, cards, you're loads of fun
You consist of red and black
All your games are played by everyone
Including gin rummy and blackjack

The face cards are the jack, queen, and king
Your funny one is the joker
Aces are wild and can mean a happy thing
Even in a game of poker

Numbered cards go down from ten to two
Those may also come in handy
Whether the deck is old or new
And are quite dandy

Each shape ranges from a diamond to a heart
They are great in each special way
Every card does their own needed part
In all games played at night or day

Either for gambling or having fun
Card decks are very good
They can be handled by anyone
As they all should

Great Poem About Billiards

Billiards, a game of many balls
Also known as pool
Has a parlor of very big halls
And is extremely cool

Solids go from one to eight
With the first colored bright
The set is truly great
While the last is as black as night

Stripes are from nine to fifteen
Which have a very long line
They're the higher ones that are keen
Along with being just as fine

Another part is the stick named a cue
The main ball for shots is plain white
Those are needs for the game all so true
That is played in full sight

The balls are lined up with a triangle rack
Winning shots are sunk in the pockets
Which are in the front, center, and back
As scores can go high like skyrockets

Great Poem Which Talks About Golf

Golf, a very popular outdoor game
Which consists of a lot of green
It has a truly wonderful name
And is considered splendid and keen

Clubs for this sport are all very fine
The woods range from one to four
The irons are marked one to nine
There is the putter that is not a bore

Obstacles include water and sand
Another is the area called the rough
Always be ready to lend a helping hand
Even this game can be very, very, tough

The fairway is known as a good part
It can serve as a somewhat useful guide
Golfers who follow it easy are very smart
As long as they are on the correct side

Lastly, there is the putting green
Which indicates the spot for the hole
Arriving there is worth being seen
Without ever paying an unnecessary toll

Poem For All Fans Of Bowling

Bowling, bowling, what a sport
Which is played by a ton
The group can be of any sort
Guaranteed to have much fun

The game is done in its alley
With people trying to get a big score
And they're meant to dally
While playing more and more

Knocking all pins down once is a strike
As a hot knife through butter
Those are truly worth a like
While shots with nothing down are a gutter

Every pin down in two rolls is a spare
That is easy or tough
It has been done everywhere
And can sometimes be rough

Whether it's competition or just fun
Bowling is a big game
Some call it number one
And can be considered of huge fame

Outstanding Poem All About Medals

All medals from far and near
Given to those who work very well
These prizes elaborate on much cheer
That are as fun as the ring of a bell

Bronze indicates everyone in rank three
Whose accomplishments are just about fair
Even their completions deserve glee
Without any amounts of despair

Silver medals are for ones in second place
Anyone who is a runner-up is not bad
Since their positions were close to an ace
And should be just as jolly and glad

Awards in gold reveal everybody on top
Who did each amount of their best
This one is never meant to stop
Which is just as good as the rest

New Poem About Weather

All weather good or bad
In its many forms
You make us happy or sad
Starting out as sun or storms

Each year begins with Spring
With occasional pouring rain
Water comes onto everything
But there are new plants we gain

Summer calls for warmth and sun
We go out with glee and play
And are meant to have much fun
That is set for every day

Fall triggers each wind and cloud
Which also means time for school
They can blow awfully loud
Making our weather somewhat cool

Winter signals bitterly cold
With lots of ice and snow
Being outside is put on hold
That tells us no way to go

New Poem About The World

Everybody lives in a country, city, or town
For what they are worth
Even if dressed in a suit or a gown
Which all come from Earth

Full of live animals and plants
7 continents that are all the lands
Everything from ferns to ants
As well as those who are human bands

The longest time on Earth is years
Consisting of 365 days
Meant for sadness or cheers
Occurring in all different ways

Shortest times are seconds, minutes, and hours
Going by all so very quick
With the weather showing its powers
Like a flame vanishing from a candle wick

Earth is way out in space
In a universe extending very long
It may always keep up its rotation and pace
Although we could be wrong

Poem For Lovers Of Australia

Australia, land of down under
Full of koala bears and the kangaroo
Continent loaded with pure wonder
And other sights, too

Find other animals such as the wallaby
Learn all about its home
Do what you can to explore with glee
And feel free to roam

Study boomerangs and their use
Throw them with caution and care
Be careful not to keep them loose
As they come from everywhere

Research this land all you can
You never know what you shall learn
Anyone will be an admirer or fan
With information to burn

Look up info on Crocodile Dundee
See what his life was like here
In Australia, be all you can be
Feel all full of great cheer

Poem Dedicated To Ireland

Dublin, Ireland called the Emerald Isle
Country full of lovely green
Guaranteed to bring out a smile
And is clearly seen

Land of leprechauns and their gold
Rainbows, rainbows, everywhere
Where the adventurers are bold
Color located here and there

Golf is the game
All irons, putters, and woods
Courses covered in green and all the same
Plenty of Irish goods

Come to Ireland for lots of luck
Plenty of shamrocks and clovers to find
Do what you can to get a fine meal of duck
Those are the ties that will bind

Travel here to the many sights
Like Shillelagh Castle and the Blarney Stone
Meant for days and nights
Which you will all treasure for your own

Fine Poem About Milk

Milk, a simply fine and delicious drink
That comes from the animal called the cow
It's very, very, tasty as everyone should think
The beverage has come a long way here and now

Most of this is in the common color, white
Another flavor is chocolate that is shown in brown
All brands of milk are considered a wonderful sight
Which is anywhere and any place around each town

Other types of these include banana and strawberry
That come out in the separate shades of pink and
yellow
Even coconut milk is meant to make you nice and
merry
As well as an extremely jolly good and happy fellow

Milk that is from every dairy, farm, and store
Will make your teeth and bones very strong
This liquid should never be called bad or sore
With all its great calcium, nothing will go wrong

Terrific Poem Which Talks About Coffee

Coffee, coffee, to start your day
People drink it either dark or light
Always have it in your own proper way
To begin every morning off just right

It can be made slowly with grinding beans
Instant coffee with water is done in the pot
The beverage is prepared in all different means
And is served nicely warm or extremely hot

Coffee can be consumed black or white
Sugar or cream help make it sweet
Even adding milk keeps it really tight
Just the exact amount of each gets it complete

The drink can be served heated or cold
Depending on the several types of brewing
This is something else that never gets old
It will be around for everyone's viewing

Great Poem About Ice Cream

Ice cream, ice cream, here and there
It's very sweet and our best delight
Endless flavors come from everywhere
Whether it's during the day or at night

You begin with vanilla, chocolate, and strawberry
More varieties are produced for days and days
Your taste is meant to make us excited and merry
By being served to everyone in many different ways

It's given to anyone either via cone or cup
Their toppings provide more sweetness and joy
Sales for this dessert can and will keep going up
Especially from each and every girl and boy

Everybody from all around loves ice cream
That is something else meant to keep us cold
It's actually true for hot days as it would seem
Which will be adored by all people young or old

Fine Poem That Talks About Bakeries

Bakeries, bakeries, everywhere
Bread, cakes, doughnuts, and other delights
Goodies from here and there
All set on our sights

Cupcakes, muffins, rolls, and tarts
Prepared by our many great cooks
Made to please and warm our hearts
Everything with good looks

Baked goods meant for all our days
Sweets made for our selection
All done in several ways
Set up to complete perfection

Bakeries, bakeries, way to go
We may adore your foods once or twice
They give us a wonderful show
With everything all dandy and nice

Keep pleasing us how you can
Even a pastry from you never fails
Little by little, you can win another popular fan
Do your best and receive many sales

All Important Poem Associated With The Five Senses

Our senses here and there
Range from sight to touch
And are meant to give us care
As we need them very much

We use our eyes to see
At distances near and far
They must be as clear as can be
To know where we are

Ears are for hearing
Several sounds soft and loud
One good noise is people cheering
A bad one is thunder from a cloud

Smelling comes from the nose
To detect all odors good or bad
One fine scent is of a rose
The smell of trash drives us mad

Taste is done with the tongue
For many different foods
Meant for the old and young
Putting them in various moods

We touch with our hands and skin
Avoid contact with all fires
A top is safe and given a spin
Never touch any electrical wires

Vital Poem About Traffic Lights

Traffic lights from all around
That alert any van, truck, or even car
Are on every street to be found
And are located near and far

Green lights indicate go
With transportation proceeding at a careful pace
Neither too fast nor too slow
Even in any wide or narrow space

Yellow lights are meant for slowing down
Vehicles can still go at a steady speed
These signals are important for all roads in every town
Only drive at the flow you really need

Red lights mean stop right away
No cars should ever try to turn
Even if green lights are in delay
That is another law you should learn

Whether it's an arrow or light
Every color means a different thing
By driving either day or night
Stay on the correct wing

Amazing Poem That
Talks About Light

Light on the Earth comes from all around
The color of our world appears from the sun
It is everywhere from the sky to the ground
Which mostly indicates time for work or fun

Other forms of this include bulbs and fire
That come from either a lamp or a candle
It also involves the use of any electrical wire
As only professionals know how to handle

Light often comes in shades of yellow or white
It tells the entire time of morning and afternoon
Much later, it gets dark and signals time of night
Which is represented by the sole light of the moon

This is something that is much needed everywhere
Everyone can and will continue saying it is always
bright
Any type of the matter should be handled with lots of
care
Without it, everything will be all out of focus and sight

Outstanding Poem About Color

Color comes from the heart
It starts with red, yellow, and blue
They are used for art
Along with other ones, too

Orange is mixed from yellow and red
Purple comes from red and blue
This about colors must be said
And green is very true

Pink is made from red and white
Which can mean a lovely day
As well as a pretty sight
While something sad is found in gray

Some ones are shiny and bright
Among these are silver and gold
They make our metal things tight
As well as very cold

There are colors all around
That make up everything
From the sky to the ground
And can make us all sing

Terrific Poem About Water

Water, water, from all around
You're here to keep us cool
It's everywhere to be found
Especially for a swimming pool

It makes up our rivers, seas, and oceans
There is even some for any type of lake
While it flows and moves in different motions
And to even help us cook, hydrate, and bake

You also come from the clouds of our rain
Water is needed to help plants and crops grow
There are even lots of flowers that we carefully gain
Whether everything rises very quickly or fairly slow

Aquatic life depends on you greatly to swim
This goes a whole lot for turtles, crabs, and fish
Without water, we would all feel completely grim
Having it incredibly handy could be our fondest wish

Composition For All Lovers Of Music

Music, music, we admire you
All your tones are fun
Whether they are happy or blue
You're heard by a ton

The instruments that play you are fine
We love you for what you are
A lot of your sound is divine
Even if it comes from near or far

Whatever forms you are played in
They can make us happy or sad
We may show a frown or grin
Hopefully, you won't always sound bad

Either done by singles or bands
Music is meant for all
It will be heard from many lands
And is also fun at a dance or ball

Each instrument will show their sound
That can be short or long
Sadness or joy can go all around
No matter what is heard in every song

Great Poem About Money

Money, money, don't go away
When vanishing, you make us blue
Your green has always made our day
And so have you

You come in coins and bills
Our destiny comes upon your sight
With you gone, it's like us taking sleeping pills
It becomes your duty to make things right

Dollar, quarter, nickel, penny, or dime
You make us smile
Always having you handy, it's our great old time
We love stacking you pile after pile

Your value has always been a treasure
We adore you for what you are
It has always been our pleasure
Whether you come from near or far

Money, money, you're ours to keep
Our lives have depended on you
Please don't go or we'll weep
That I say is definitely true

You will always be for who is needy
Poor ones will rely on you
Never be with those who are greedy
Common people speak all this, too

Amazing Poem About The Lottery

The lottery from every state is our biggest prize
There are many different amounts to win
Money won from here is in any size
Hitting the jackpot can indicate a huge grin

Odds for this are millions to one
Various tickets are played each day
Every variety can trigger much fun
Those who win big can yell hooray

All moments with these releases a load of cash
People celebrate with victory and cheer
Along with running out in a quick flash
Whether they come from far or near

Winning the lottery is meant for many joys
It will be spread out day and night
For all men, ladies, girls, and boys
And is considered a very happy sight

Great Poem About Poems

Any and all poetry is everywhere to be found
Words in every line make us happy or sad
Reading and hearing it triggers any feeling or sound
Whether they are surprisingly good or awfully bad

Each one written is meant to rhyme differently or the
same
There is no limit to the number of words in each
dictated line
Their topics are about pretty much anything including
a game
Every poem that is composed with care can and will
sound just fine

Themes in any of these will come out as either old or
new
Writing poems does require lots of patience as well as
skill
That which I say about successful poetry is all so very
true
Anyone can develop great talent for this and
eventually will

No matter what the topic or subject is in any one or
more poems
Writing as many as possible could be considered a
very lovely art
Many people can come up with a lot of these in their
own homes
And will always be something big meant to warm
everyone's heart

www.ingramcontent.com/pod-product-compliance
Lightning Source LLC
Chambersburg PA
CBHW051236120626
46547CB00013B/1663